ALTERNATOR
BOOKS™

THE AMERICAN INDIAN RIGHTS MOVEMENT

ERIC BRAUN

Lerner Publications ◆ Minneapolis

Content Consultant: Jill Doerfler (White Earth Anishinaabe), Associate
Professor of American Indian Studies, University of Minnesota–
Duluth

Lerner Publications Company
A division of Lerner Publishing Group, Inc.
241 First Avenue North
Minneapolis, MN 55401 USA

For reading levels and more information, look up this title at
www.lernerbooks.com.

Main body text set in Aptifer Slab LT Pro Regular 11.5/18.
Typeface provided by Linotype AG.

Library of Congress Cataloging-in-Publication Data

Names: Braun, Eric, 1971– author.
Title: The American Indian Rights Movement / Eric Braun.
Description: Minneapolis : Lerner Publications, [2019] | Series:
    Movements that matter | Includes bibliographical references and
    index. | Audience: Grades 4–6. | Audience: Ages 8–12.
Identifiers: LCCN 2017050332 (print) | LCCN 2017050676 (ebook) |
    ISBN 9781541525559 (eb) | ISBN 9781541523333 (library bound : alk.
    paper)
Subjects: LCSH: Indians of North America—Government relations—
    Juvenile literature. | Indians of North America—Civil rights—
    Juvenile literature. | Indians of North America—Legal status, laws,
    etc.—Juvenile literature. | American Indian Movement—Juvenile
    literature. | Indians, Treatment of—United States—Juvenile
    literature.
Classification: LCC E93 (ebook) | LCC E93 .B78 2019 (print) |
    DDC 323.1197—dc23

LC record available at https://lccn.loc.gov/2017050332

Manufactured in the United States of America
2-47056-34665-12/28/2018

CONTENTS

INTRODUCTION

#NODAPL

It's late September 2016, and more than a thousand people are gathered at an American Indian prayer camp. They've come to **protest** the construction of the Dakota Access Pipeline (DAPL) through sacred Standing Rock Sioux tribal grounds and across the tribe's main source of drinking water. Behind the crowd, a string of concrete construction barriers is spray-painted with the words "No DAPL." The crowd has grown since the protest began in early April, partly due to a social media campaign using the hashtag #NoDAPL.

Protesters, calling themselves water protectors, held prayer circles and actively blocked construction on the pipeline.

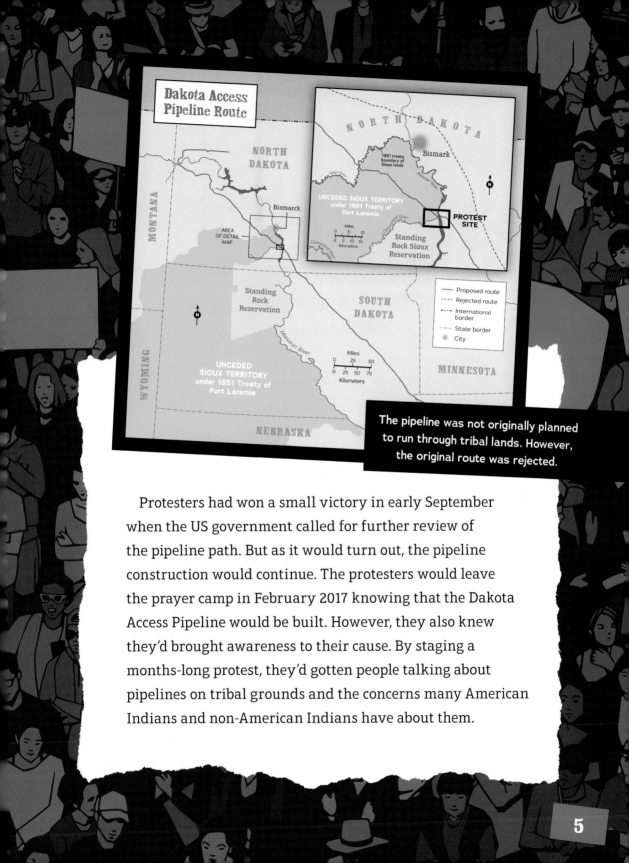

Dakota Access Pipeline Route

NORTH DAKOTA

MONTANA

Bismarck

AREA OF DETAIL MAP

Standing Rock Reservation

SOUTH DAKOTA

WYOMING

Missouri River

UNCEDED SIOUX TERRITORY under 1851 Treaty of Fort Laramie

NEBRASKA

MINNESOTA

NORTH DAKOTA

1851 treaty boundary of Sioux lands

Bismark

Heart River

Missouri River

UNCEDED SIOUX TERRITORY under 1851 Treaty of Fort Laramie

Cannonball River

Cannonball River

Miles
0   5   10

0   5   10   15
Kilometers

PROTEST SITE

Standing Rock Sioux Reservation

N

—— Proposed route
- - - Rejected route
-··- International border
-···- State border
● City

Miles
0   25   50

0   25   50   75
Kilometers

The pipeline was not originally planned to run through tribal lands. However, the original route was rejected.

Protesters had won a small victory in early September when the US government called for further review of the pipeline path. But as it would turn out, the pipeline construction would continue. The protesters would leave the prayer camp in February 2017 knowing that the Dakota Access Pipeline would be built. However, they also knew they'd brought awareness to their cause. By staging a months-long protest, they'd gotten people talking about pipelines on tribal grounds and the concerns many American Indians and non-American Indians have about them.

CHAPTER 1
FIGHTING FOR NATIVE RIGHTS

The #NoDAPL protests are just one event in a long history of the American Indian rights movement. For hundreds of years, the United States took away land and rights from American Indians. But American Indians have always fought against mistreatment.

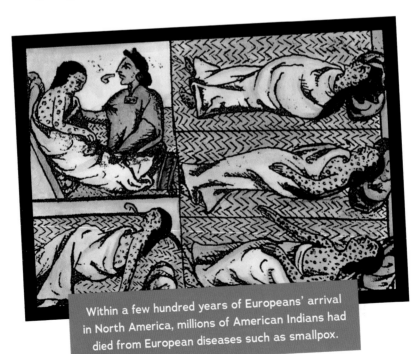

Within a few hundred years of Europeans' arrival in North America, millions of American Indians had died from European diseases such as smallpox.

THE LOSS OF RIGHTS

When the United States became its own nation, the US government considered American Indian tribes to be **sovereign** nations. The US government made formal agreements and signed **treaties** to purchase land from American Indian tribes. However, soon the US government began disregarding the law and forcing American Indians to move to **reservations** and other specific areas, where the land was often of low quality. US laws and acts stripped American Indians of their rights.

Throughout the nineteench and early twentieth centuries, American Indians were often denied basic rights. They were not even allowed to travel off their home reservations.

Removing American Indian children from their communities and placing them in boarding schools actively prevented them from learning about their cultures.

The United States tried to make American Indians give up their traditional beliefs and practice Christian traditions. Many American Indian children were taken from their parents and sent to boarding schools designed to **assimilate** them. Despite these efforts, many American Indians resisted and continued to practice their cultures and traditions.

A GROWING MOVEMENT

In 1924 all American Indians were granted US citizenship through the Snyder Act. They also retained the citizenship of their tribal nations. Despite having US citizenship, many American Indians continued to face discrimination and difficulty practicing their cultures.

By the 1960s, organized groups of American Indians were fighting for their peoples' rights. In 1968 the American Indian Movement (AIM) was founded in Minneapolis, Minnesota, to combat police mistreatment. Soon, new AIM chapters formed in cities across the United States.

President Calvin Coolidge (*center*) signed the Snyder Act into law on June 2, 1924. Despite the law, American Indians were not allowed to vote. Some even claimed that the act was another attempt at promoting assimilation.

CHAPTER 2

PROTESTING FOR RIGHTS

The American Indian rights movement grew quickly in the late 1960s and 1970s. American Indian **activists** began to hold large public protests to bring attention to issues facing American Indians, including the unique issue of treaty rights and cultural rights.

American Indian Movement leaders Russell Means (*seated with feathers*) and Dennis Banks (*seated with vest*) rallied members of their communities to support AIM causes.

EDUCATION ISSUES

AIM worked to create schools where American Indian children could learn about their own history, languages, and cultures in an environment that was safe for the children and that valued the opinions of their parents. The movement called for an end to what it said was poor treatment of American Indians by the US government, the public, and the police. In 1970 the National Indian Education Association (NIEA) formed to fight for better educational opportunities for American Indian students.

The National Indian Education Association formed as a response to a growing discussion about how to meet the needs of educators, students, and American Indian communities.

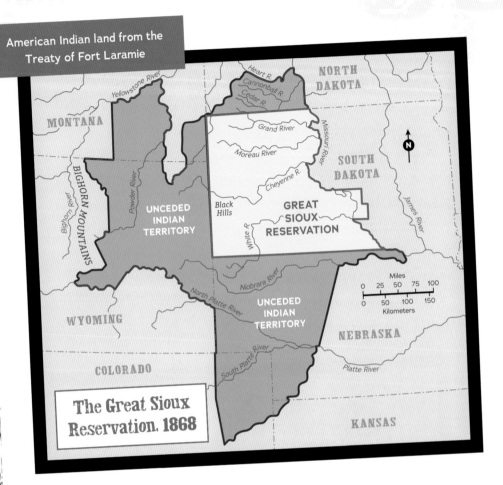

The Great Sioux Reservation, 1868

LAND ISSUES

Another big concern was the rights of American Indian tribes to land. Activists wanted the government to honor the treaties it signed with tribes years earlier, and they used public **occupations** to bring attention to this cause.

For example, in 1868 the United States signed the Treaty of Fort Laramie, which established the Great Sioux

Reservation. This land included the sacred Black Hills. In 1877, after gold had been discovered in the Black Hills, the United States broke the treaty and took the land.

The government mined there before making the land a national park. They built the Mount Rushmore National Memorial. In the early 1970s, several groups of American Indian activists occupied Mount Rushmore, demanding the return of the land to the Lakota people, who were the true owners of the Great Sioux Reservation based on the Treaty of Fort Laramie. This bold step brought public awareness to American Indian rights.

Mount Rushmore was carved into the side of a sacred site that the Lakota people called Six Grandfathers.

Indians of All Tribes members occupied Alcatraz Island for more than nineteen months. They wanted the island to become an American Indian cultural center and school.

Around then a group called Indians of All Tribes occupied Alcatraz Island in California. The group took over the island from 1969 to 1971 and demanded that the US government turn over land that it had promised to a tribe in an 1868 treaty.

A few years later, in 1973, the American Indian Movement organized an occupation of Wounded Knee, the site of the 1890 massacre of about three hundred Lakota by US soldiers. They demanded that the government hold hearings on many treaties the United States had broken.

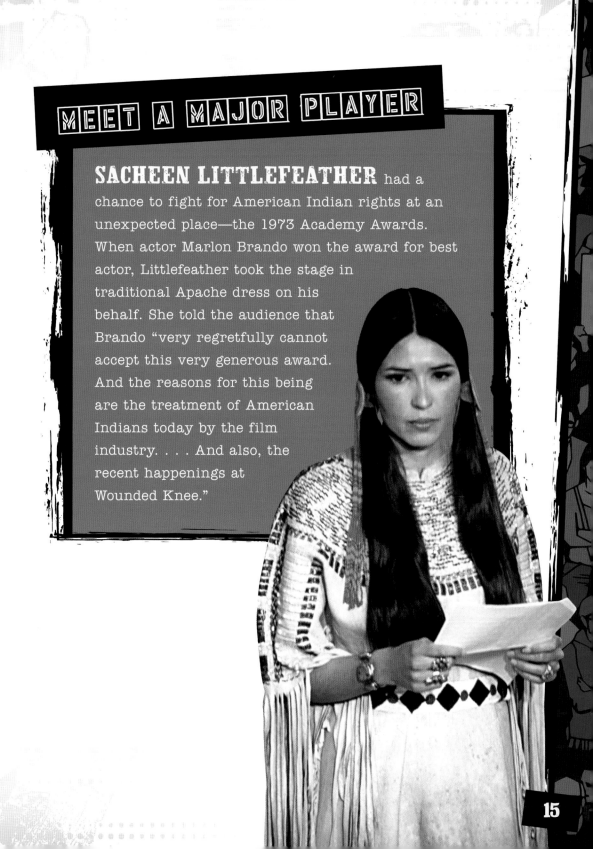

SACHEEN LITTLEFEATHER had a chance to fight for American Indian rights at an unexpected place—the 1973 Academy Awards. When actor Marlon Brando won the award for best actor, Littlefeather took the stage in traditional Apache dress on his behalf. She told the audience that Brando "very regretfully cannot accept this very generous award. And the reasons for this being are the treatment of American Indians today by the film industry. . . . And also, the recent happenings at Wounded Knee."

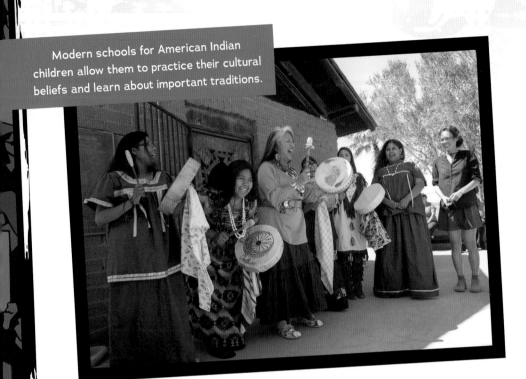

Modern schools for American Indian children allow them to practice their cultural beliefs and learn about important traditions.

SEEING RESULTS

The protests and occupations of the 1970s brought public attention to issues facing American Indians. Although the government rarely returned land, American Indian activists did make some progress toward the recognition of treaty, education, and social rights, as well as religious freedom. In 1972 the Indian Education Act reaffirmed the government's responsibility to meet the education needs of American Indians. In 1976 the Indian Health Care Improvement Act provided better funding for American Indian health care. And in 1978, the Indian Child Welfare Act recognized the rights of tribes regarding their children.

Also in 1978, the American Indian Religious Freedom Act recognized the right of American Indians to believe and practice their traditional religions.

THE LONGEST WALK

However, not all laws proposed in the 1970s were good for American Indians. Some threatened their way of life. In 1978 activists fought against eleven anti-American Indian bills. To protest, they held a spiritual walk called the Longest Walk. Protesters walked for five months from San Francisco to Washington, DC, with about two thousand protesters coming together at the end.

Once the walkers reached Washington, DC, they staged public protests and tribal

The Longest Walk protested legislation that would close tribal schools and hospitals, limit hunting and fishing rights, and restrict tribal government.

ceremonies. None of the bills passed Congress. And people across the country learned more about American Indian culture and issues of poverty and treaty rights.

A Moment in the Movement

Long protest marches were not new to the American Indian rights movement at the time of the Longest Walk. In October 1972, hundreds of American Indian activists began a weeks-long journey to Washington, DC. They called their protest the Trail of Broken Treaties. Their goals were to highlight unfair treatment of American Indians and to protest the proposed cuts in the budget of the Bureau of Indian Affairs (BIA), which is the government office that oversees all American Indian lands for the United States.

The protesters had prepared a Twenty-Point Position Paper of demands. When government officials refused to meet them, the protesters began an occupation of the BIA building. The protest lasted about one week, and in the end, the US government agreed to some of the activists' demands.

CHAPTER 3
EXPANDING THE MOVEMENT

Once the American Indian rights movement gained public attention in the 1970s, it continued to grow. Over the next decades, activists continued to focus on securing treaty rights as well as combating poverty. They also took on the issues of cultural pride and wider environmental health.

Some popular children's books and movies, such as *Peter Pan*, released in 1953, have been criticized for misrepresenting American Indians and their cultures. Such imagery perpetuates harmful stereotypes.

A Moment in the Movement

In 1992 activists staged a massive Columbus Day protest in San Francisco at the five hundredth anniversary of Columbus landing in America. They were critical of the story that Christopher Columbus discovered a land that was already inhabited. Protesters interrupted the celebration by blocking the bay to prevent a Columbus-themed boat from entering under the Golden Gate Bridge. They also threw eggs at parade floats.

These activists were instrumental in the cause to change how Americans think about US history. The same year as the Columbus Day protests, Berkeley, California, became the first US city to officially celebrate Indigenous Peoples' Day instead of Columbus Day. More than fifty towns and cities now officially celebrate the holiday, which honors America's original inhabitants.

SPORTS TEAMS AND MASCOTS

One very public battle American Indians took on was combating the use of American Indian stereotypes in popular culture, especially in American sports. Both school and professional teams have used stereotypes and racial slurs for their team names, mascots, or logos. As early as the 1960s, organizations such as the National Congress of American Indians were calling attention to stereotyping of American Indian cultures in the media. But the 1990s saw a growth in the movement as American Indian rights activists strengthened their call for an end to this stereotyping. Many schools responded by changing their team names and racist mascots. Professional sports have been slower to respond. Some professional sports teams still have American Indian–themed names and mascots.

American Indians use the hashtag #NotYourMascot to continue to raise awareness about inappropriate mascots and team names.

RUSSELL MEANS was an Oglala Lakota American Indian activist who became the national head of the American Indian Movement. He participated in the Alcatraz Island occupation in 1969 and was one of the leaders of a 1971 Mount Rushmore occupation. For the next forty years, Means was at the forefront of the American Indian rights movement. In the 1990s, he also became a successful actor and producer, starring in films and television shows. He helped promote more positive depictions of American Indians in popular culture. Means fought for American Indian rights until his death in 2012.

American Indian and other environmental protesters are concerned about the potential health impact of oil pipelines on both human and animal lives.

PROTECTING THE ENVIRONMENT

In recent years, other activist groups have joined American Indians in a fight to protect the environment. In the early 2010s, activists joined together to protest the planned construction of a leg of the nearly 1,200-mile (1,930 km) Keystone XL oil pipeline. They were protesting the pipeline's path through tribal lands and were worried about the pipeline's impact on the environment. They wanted the US government to delay construction and study the environmental impact of the pipeline.

Protesters succeeded in bringing public attention to the issue and getting further studies. In 2015 President Barack Obama used his veto power to block the project. However, two years later, President Donald Trump signed an order for the construction to continue.

Hundreds of protesters gathered outside the White House after Trump approved the continued construction of the Keystone XL pipeline.

CHAPTER 4

THE FUTURE

The American Indian rights movement has achieved many milestones. But American Indians continue to face major obstacles. About 27 percent of American Indians live in poverty. And a greater number than that are unemployed, especially on reservations where unemployment is often 50 percent. And Native Peoples in the United States are policed more severely than the general population and imprisoned at a much higher rate.

The Department of Housing and Urban Development helps fund housing on reservations. However, despite treaties and governmental agreements, reservation housing has been historically underfunded.

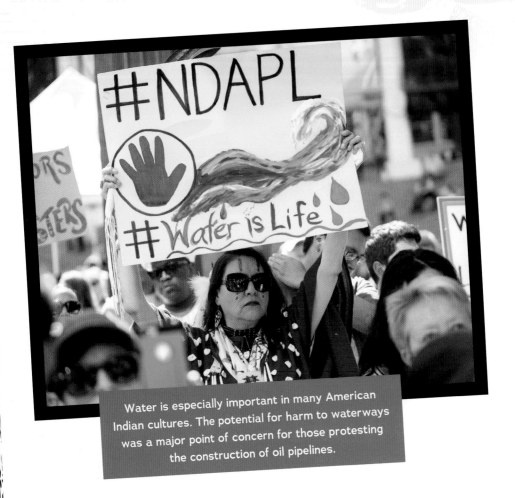

Water is especially important in many American Indian cultures. The potential for harm to waterways was a major point of concern for those protesting the construction of oil pipelines.

Yet American Indians continue to fight for important causes. For example, the Nibi Water Walk Movement started in 2003. Anishinaabe elder Josephine Mandamin decided to walk around Lake Superior because she was concerned about water pollution. In Anishinaabe culture, women have a responsibility to pray for and protect the water. The movement grew quickly, and there have been many Nibi Water Walks including at all the Great Lakes as well as the Ohio, Saint Louis, and Missouri Rivers.

American Indians continue to face discrimination despite their fight for their rights and the land. These issues are likely to continue until more people gain a greater understanding of American Indian rights. But until then, activists are prepared to continue fighting for their causes.

The American Indian rights movement is still fighting for equal and respectful treatment. In the spring of 2017, members of several tribes joined together to successfully call for the removal of a sculpture inspired by the 1862 massacre of thirty-eight American Indian men in Minnesota.

Timeline

1500s: European explorers arrive in North America, home to millions of Native Peoples.

1776: The founders of the United States recognize American Indian tribes as independent nations and make many treaties with them.

1800s: The United States breaks treaties and forces thousands of American Indians to relocate from their homelands to reservations.

1830: The Indian Removal Act allows the US government to take land away from American Indians.

1924: American Indians are all given US citizenship but retain citizenship in their American Indian nation.

1965: American Indians gain the right to vote under the Voting Rights Act.

1968: The Indian Civil Rights Act guarantees American Indians many of the same rights guaranteed to other Americans in the US Constitution's Bill of Rights.

The American Indian Movement (AIM) is founded in Minneapolis, Minnesota, and quickly spreads to other cities.

1969: Indians of All Tribes begins a nearly two-year occupation of Alcatraz Island to protest government violation of treaty rights.

1970: The National Indian Education Association forms.

1970–1971: American Indian activists stage several occupations of the Mount Rushmore National Memorial.

1972: The weeks-long Trail of Broken Treaties march takes place to highlight unfair treatment of American Indians.

1973: About two hundred American Indian protesters occupy Wounded Knee, the site of the 1890 massacre of about three hundred Lakota by US soldiers.

Sacheen Littlefeather declines Marlon Brando's Academy Award for best actor.

1978: The five-month Longest Walk between San Francisco and Washington, DC, takes place.

The American Indian Religious Freedom Act protects the rights of American Indians to believe in and practice their traditional religious ceremonies.

1992: Protesters disturb San Francisco's Columbus Day celebration, and Berkeley, California, becomes the first US city to celebrate Indigenous Peoples' Day.

2002: President George W. Bush signs an executive order reaffirming the United States' commitment to tribally controlled colleges and universities.

2003: The Nibi Water Walk Movement begins when Anishinaabe elder Josephine Mandamin walks around Lake Superior.

2015: American Indian protests of the Keystone XL pipeline help lead to President Obama's veto of the project.

2016: Protesters near the Standing Rock Indian Reservation in North Dakota bring worldwide attention to the controversial construction of the Dakota Access Pipeline.

2017: President Trump signs orders to continue the Keystone XL pipeline and Dakota Access Pipeline projects.

Source Note

15   "43 Years Later, Native American Activist Sacheen Littlefeather Reflects on Rejecting Marlon Brando's Oscar," *Women in the World*, February 27, 2016, https://womenintheworld.com/2016/02/27/43-years-later-native-american-activist-reflects-on-rejecting-marlon-brandos-oscar/.

Glossary

activists: people who work to bring about social or political change

assimilate: to force individuals to absorb into the cultural tradition of a population or group

occupations: protests where people gather in one building or site and refuse to leave until their demands are met

protest: an event where people gather to express disapproval of something. Also, the act of taking part in such an event.

reservations: areas of land set aside for a special purpose, especially in North America for American Indians

sovereign: independent and with the right to rule itself

treaties: formal agreements between two or more political authorities (such as a tribe and the US government)

Further Information

American Indian Movement
https://www.aimovement.org

Erdrich, Louise. *Makoons*. New York: Harper, 2016.

Lowry, Linda. *Native Peoples of the Plains*. Minneapolis: Lerner Publications, 2017.

Machajewski, Sarah. *American Indian Rights Movement*. New York: PowerKids, 2017.

Morlock, Theresa. *Inside the Native American Rights Movement*. New York: Gareth Stevens, 2018.

National Geographic Society: Native Americans
https://www.nationalgeographic.org/topics/native-americans/

Nibi Walk
http://www.nibiwalk.org

Robertson, Joanne. *The Water Walker*. Toronto: Second Story, 2017.

Standing Rock Sioux Tribe
https://www.standingrock.org

Index

Photo Acknowledgments

The images in this book are used with the permission of: Natasha Dangond/Polaris/
Newscom, p. 4; Laura Westlund/Independent Picture Service, pp. 5, 12; Sarin Images/
The Granger Collection, New York, p. 6; Buyenlarge/Archive Photos/Getty Images, p. 7;
Library of Congress (LC-USZ62-124294), p. 8; Library of Congress (LC-USZ62-111409), p. 9;
Bettmann/Getty Images, pp. 10, 14; Joe Amon/Denver Post/Getty Images, p. 11; Everett
Collection/Newscom, p. 13; Michael Ochs Archives/Getty Images, p. 15; DAVID MCNEW/
AFP/Getty Images, p. 16; Wally McNamee/Corbis Historical/Getty Images, p. 17; © Walt
Disney Pictures/Courtesy Everett Collection, p. 20; Hannah Foslien/Getty Images,
p. 21; Kevin Winter/Getty Images, p. 22; Justin Sullivan/Getty Images, p. 23; NICHOLAS
KAMM/AFP/Getty Images, p. 24; William F. Campbell /The LIFE Images Collection/Getty
Images, p. 25; Diego G Diaz/Shutterstock.com, p. 26; ZUMA Press/Alamy Stock Photo,
p. 27. Design: Stephen Rees/Shutterstock.com (torn edges border); Amitofo/Shutterstock.
com (crowds); Milan M/Shutterstock.com (grunge frame); Miloje/Shutterstock.com
(texture background); rob zs/Shutterstock.com (protests); Kair/Shutterstock.com (raised
fist title treatment).

Front cover: Kim Komenich/The LIFE Images Collection/Getty Images (top); Bettmann/
Getty Images (left); ROBYN BECK/AFP/Getty Images (bottom); miker/Shutterstock.com
(right).